THERE WAS AN OLD LADY WHO SWALLOWED A SHELL!

by Lucille Colandro
Illustrated by Jared Lee

SCHOLASTIC INC.
Cartwheel BOOKS®

New York Toronto London Auckland Sydney
Mexico City New Delhi Hong Kong Buenos Aires

With love to Aunt Grace and Aunt Connie
— L.C.

To my daughter, Jennifer, who brightens my day
— J.L.

ISBN 0-439-81536-3

Text copyright © 2006 by Lucille Santarelli.
Illustrations copyright © 2006 by Jared Lee.
All rights reserved. Published by Scholastic Inc.
SCHOLASTIC, CARTWHEEL BOOKS, and associated logos are
trademarks and/or registered trademarks of Scholastic Inc.

12 11 10   8 9 10 11/0

Printed in the U.S.A.
First printing, May 2006

There was an old lady who swallowed a shell.
I don't know why she swallowed the shell.
She didn't tell.

There was an old lady who swallowed a crab.
Why did she grab that crawling crab?

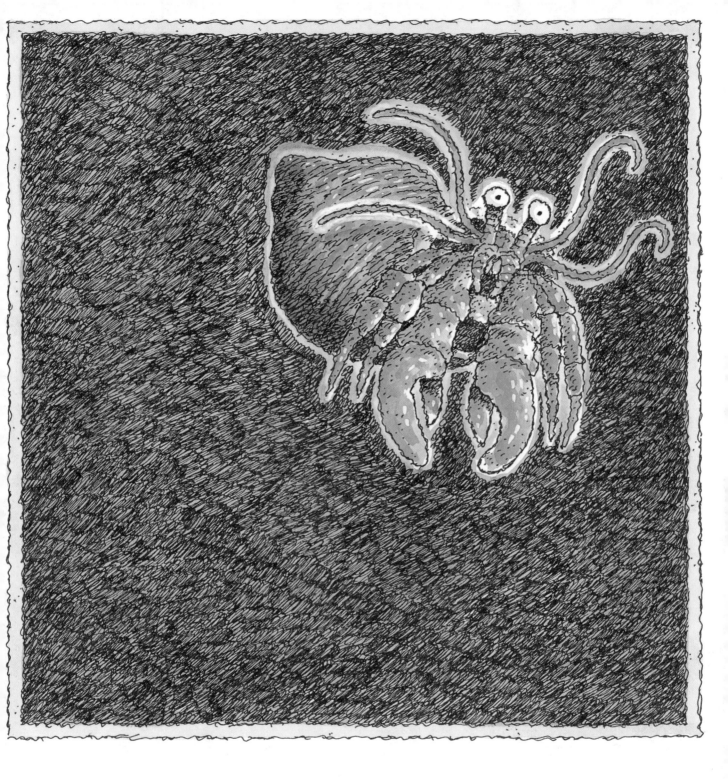

She swallowed the crab to live in the shell.
I don't know why she swallowed the shell.
She didn't tell.

There was an old lady who swallowed a fish.

What a tickly dish, that swimming fish!

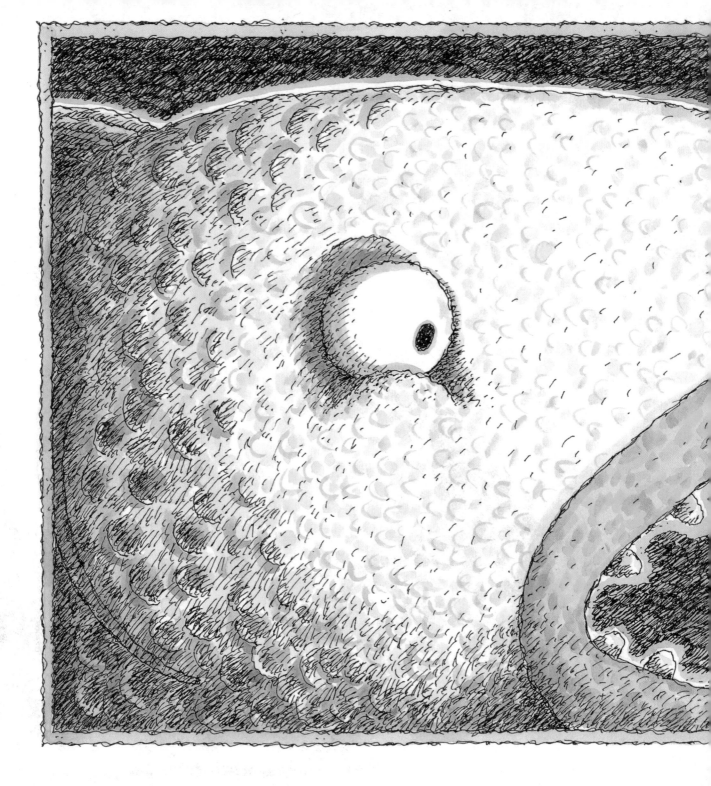

She swallowed the fish to catch the crab.
She swallowed the crab to live in the shell.

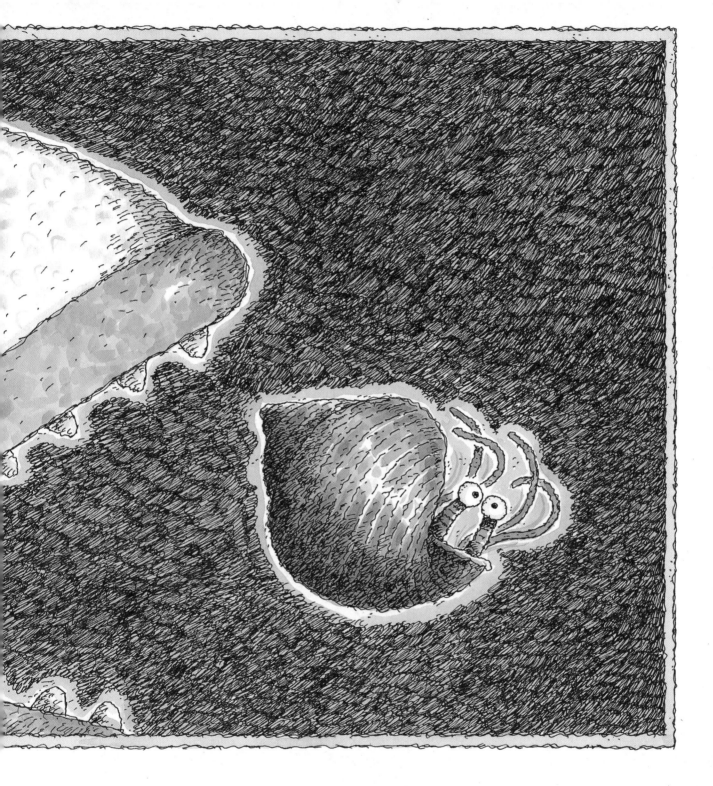

I don't know why she swallowed the shell.
She didn't tell.

There was an old lady who swallowed a gull.

It wasn't dull to swallow a gull.

She swallowed the gull to scoop up the fish.
She swallowed the fish to catch the crab.
She swallowed the crab to live in the shell.

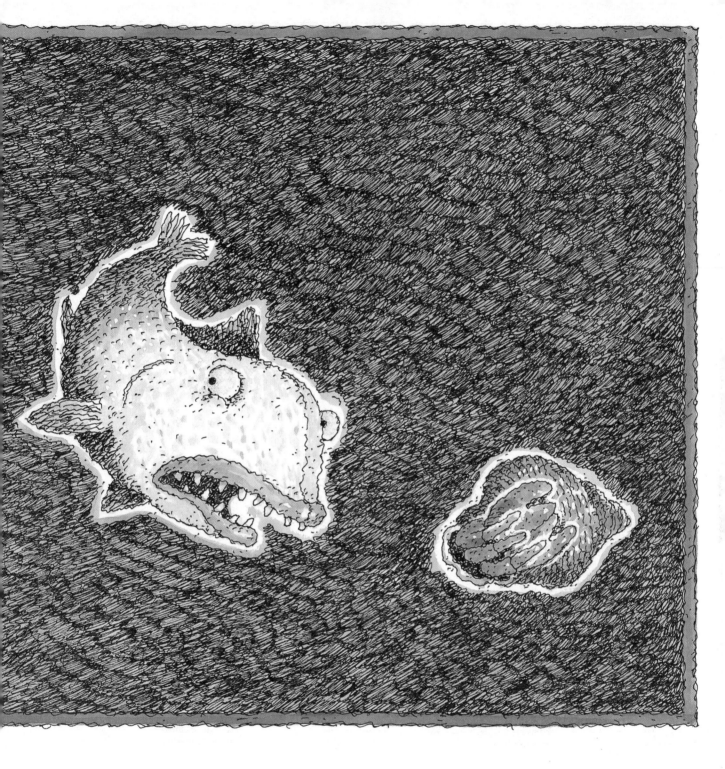

I don't know why she swallowed the shell.
She didn't tell.

There was an old lady who swallowed a pail.

She didn't wail when she swallowed the pail.

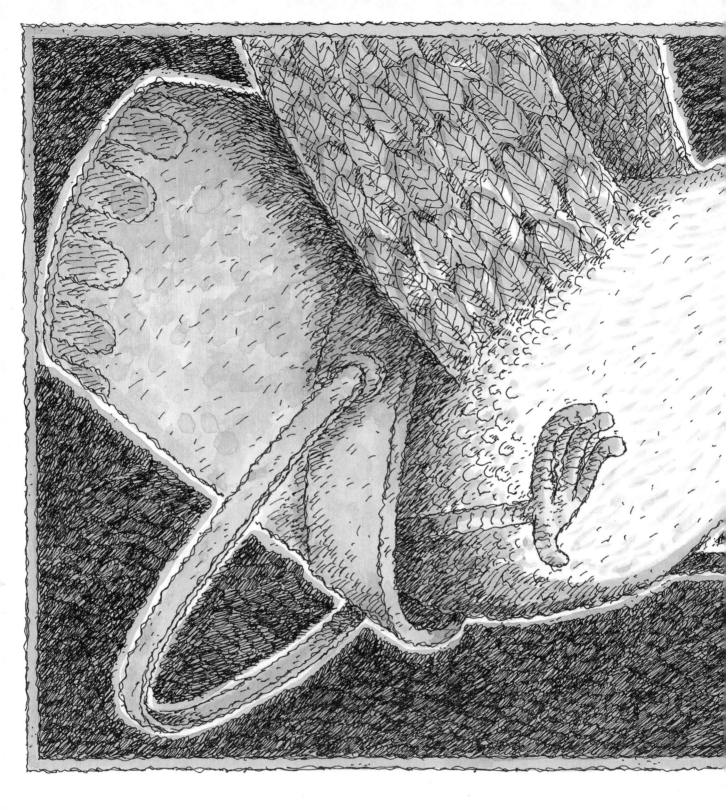

She swallowed the pail to carry the gull.

She swallowed the gull to scoop up the fish.

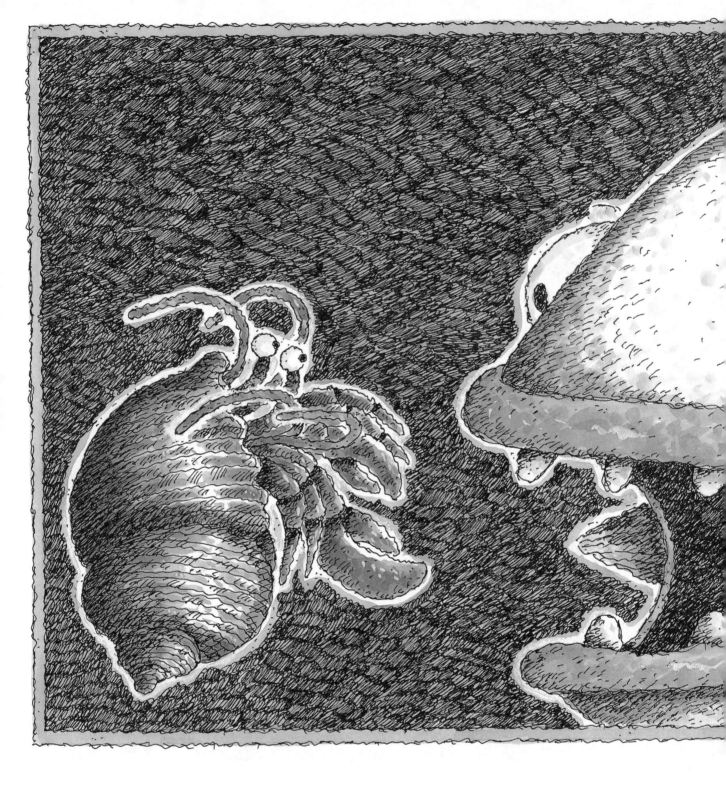

She swallowed the fish to catch the crab.
She swallowed the crab to live in the shell.

I don't know why she swallowed the shell.
She didn't tell.

There was an old lady who swallowed some sand.

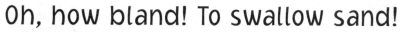

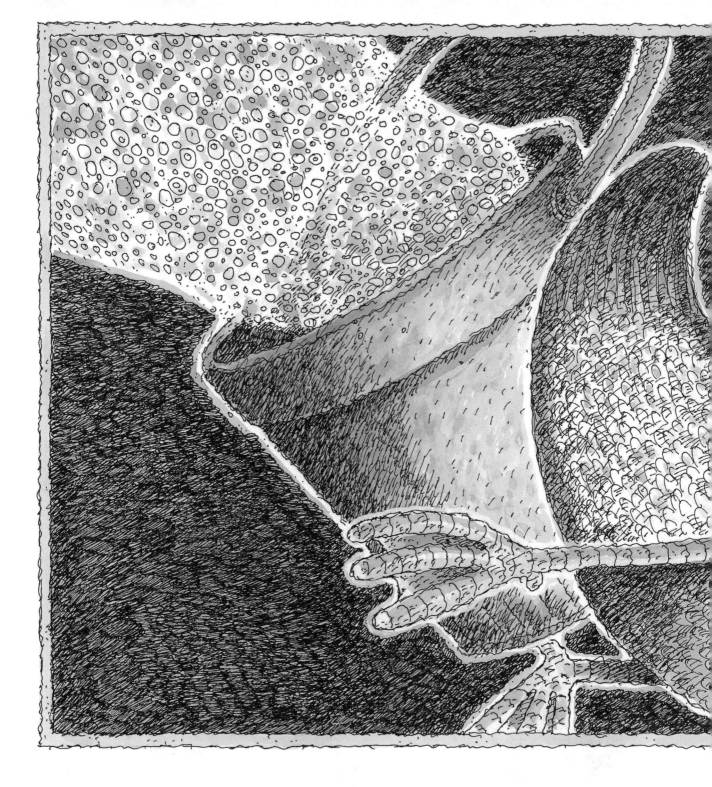

She swallowed the sand to fill up the pail.

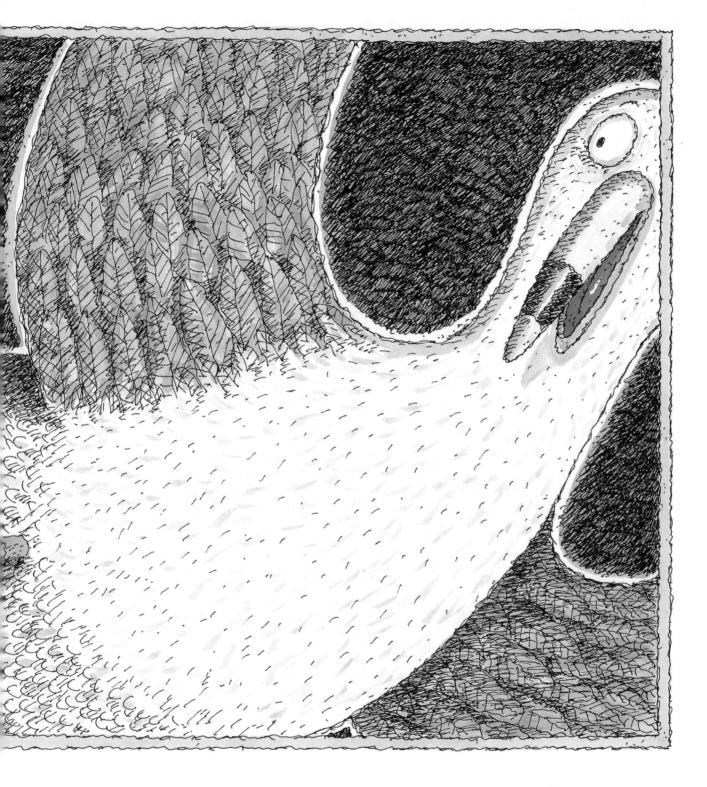

She swallowed the pail to carry the gull.

She swallowed the gull to scoop up the fish.

She swallowed the fish to catch the crab.

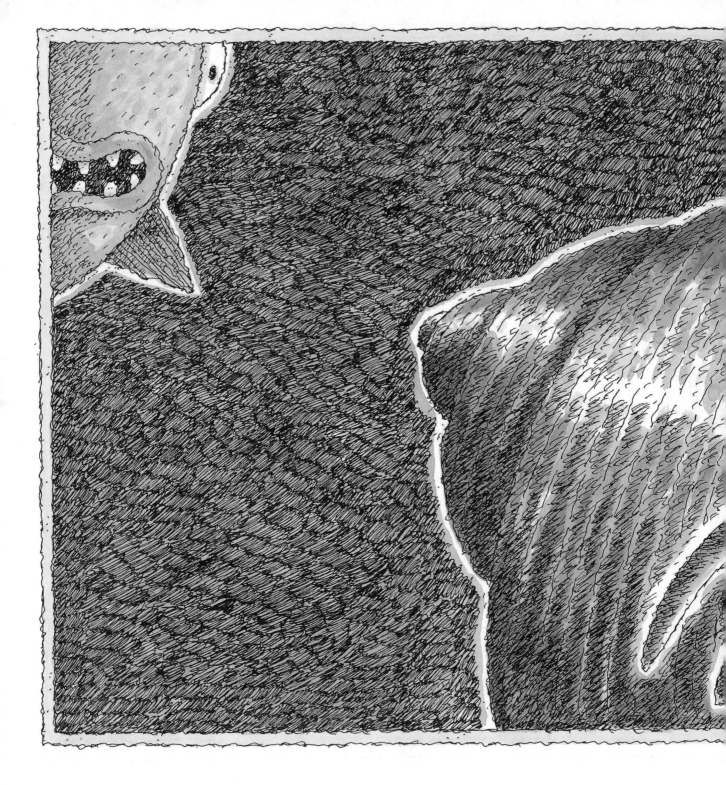

She swallowed the crab to live in the shell.

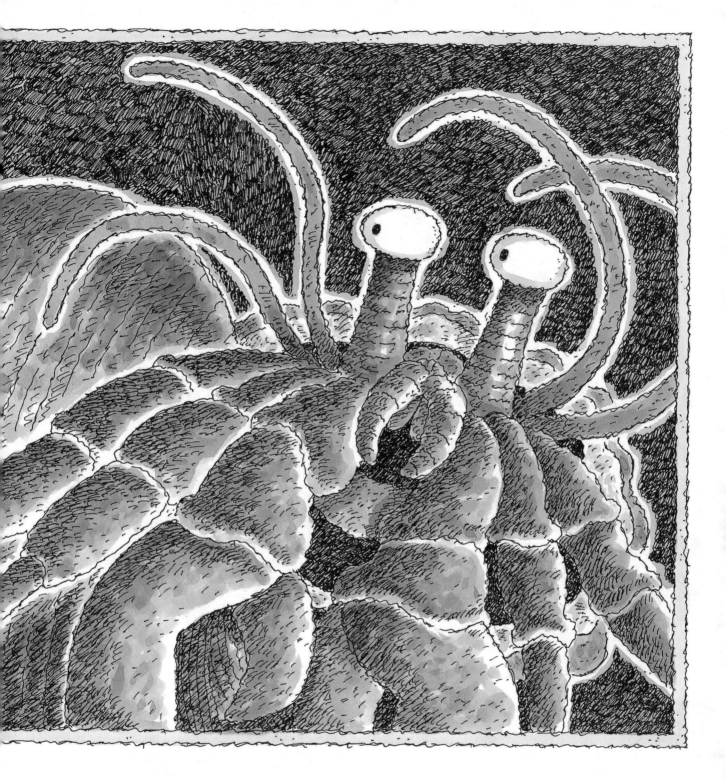

But I don't know why she swallowed the shell.
She didn't tell.

There was an old lady who swallowed a wave.

Swallowing a wave was such a big hassle,

that she suddenly burped . . .

and built a sand castle!